By the LIGHT of a STAR

TRUE CHRISTMAS STORIES

By the Light of a Star

True Christmas Stories

Anita Stansfield, Lynn C. Jaynes,
Gale Sears, Joni Hilton, Kerry Blair,
and Marilynne Todd Linford

Covenant Communications, Inc.

Cover image: *Christmas Scroll* © Sam Alfano, courtesy of iStock.

Cover design copyrighted 2008 by Covenant Communications, Inc.

Published by Covenant Communications, Inc.
American Fork, Utah

Printed in Canada
First Printing: October 2008

14 13 12 11 10 09 08 10 9 8 7 6 5 4 3 2 1

ISBN 10: 1-59811-406-9
ISBN 13: 978-1-59811-406-5

Peace on Earth

LYNN C. JAYNES

"Come on kids, let's go find a Christmas tree!" I was more than a little excited to take my young children on their very first Christmas-tree hunt. I couldn't understand why my husband, Fred, didn't share my enthusiasm. Where was his sense of fun? Of tradition?

I have great memories of Christmas-tree hunting as a child. Okay, well, really only one memory—but it's a great one. It isn't great in the sense of being Hallmark-card perfect, nor one where I hum "Over the River and Through the Woods" whenever the memory goes sleighing through my brain. It isn't even one I'd bring up during a nostalgic moment at a family function (but that's mostly because it would just start yet another tedious argument). The Christmas-tree hunt I recall was only great in the sense that I found a little corner of peace and tranquility in an otherwise very tumultuous holiday scene—and, really, that was just a dadgum miracle. The memory was so dear to my heart that for years Christmas-tree hunting was one of my "sacred cows," a tradition that I wanted to somehow re-create for my children and grandchildren. A tradition nobody had better mess with.

My great Christmas-tree hunting memory focuses on the day my family and our friends the Williamses loaded up in . . . in vehicles of some sort—Jeeps maybe, probably pickups, although ours could have been a Suburban (frankly, at seven years old it's hard to sort those things out). Anyway, there was a bunch of us kids, parents, and tagalongs piled into these vehicles, fully padded in all our winter gear so that we looked like sumo wrestlers—very modestly dressed sumo wrestlers. It's just as well no one wore seat belts in those days, because they never would have fit around us, and there never would have been enough of them anyway. But all that aside, we were headed for the South Hills to find Christmas trees.

The South Hills had tons of pine trees, but they were mostly lodgepole pines. Lodgepoles do not make good Christmas trees, because the limbs don't start for about fifteen feet off the ground. Our original plan was to trek all over the hills looking for a decent subalpine fir. The revised plan followed, which was to trek to the first subalpine fir near the spot on the road where the Jeep/pickup/Suburban had become wedged fender-high in a snowdrift. I don't know if we had four-wheel drive or not, but it wouldn't have mattered. Four-wheel drive only meant Dad tried to drive through BIGGER drifts, BIGGER mud holes, and BIGGER creek bogs. The result was always the same with or without four-wheel drive, so I never really understood the point of it.

"Okay," Dad told Mom, "put it in first gear and we'll push." My mother was a small, five-foot woman who could barely reach the gas pedal.

"Ready? One, two, three!" With that, the engine revved and my dad and anyone else who was big enough to be useful pushed and pushed and pushed. Snow went flying everywhere—all to no avail. After that, there were several shovels involved, huffing and puffing, and people barking out orders (as though someone were listening). Then the process was repeated. "Ready? One, two, three!" Again, no progress. By this time, the wet, huffing men and adolescents were not very cheerful.

I wasn't terribly inconvenienced by the ordeal. After all, the picnic box was in the backseat with me—a pot of chili, boxes of saltines, and chocolate cupcakes with nuts (I remember the menu really well). I just let all this peripheral commotion be just that—peripheral. The events outside the car were mildly interesting, but I went with the flow and let it all happen without my interference. I figured we'd be spending a good deal of time right where we were, and that would mean that we didn't have to stumble around in sumo suits looking for trees—none of which would be "wow enough" anyway—and feeling the cold sink into the roots of our teeth. As long as most of the crew was outside pushing, no one would be sitting on top of me or jabbing an elbow into my cheek, and anyway, no one was going to miss a few walnuts from the tops of those cupcakes or the frosting that hung over the edges (where all frosting is free for the snitching). So while most everyone was blaming each other for not bringing shovels or not pushing hard enough, I found a little piece of heaven in the backseat with the picnic box.

Good things can't last forever, though, and soon enough my dad came to the driver's door, opened it, reached across my mother's lap, and jammed the gearshift around, exclaiming, "You had it in reverse!" Of course everyone teased her endlessly afterward, but at that moment—trust me—no one was laughing.

Years later, it was this one memory of Christmas-tree hunting that propelled me into dragging my own kids out into the snow to hunt for a Christmas tree. But memory is a funny thing; I had not even tried to analyze my cherished memory to understand exactly why it was a good one. I just knew I wanted to take my kids Christmas-tree hunting, because that's what people do and because somehow I had a good memory tied up with Christmas-tree hunting. Oh, how I wish I had scrutinized that memory a little more carefully before trying it out. "They're gonna hate it," Fred said.

"No, you'll see. They'll love it."

"They'll hate it."

"They'll love it. *You'll* hate it."

"I'll hate it," he agreed.

"You hate a lot of things."

Fred wouldn't budge. He was not going to drive over fifty miles for a Christmas tree with a pickup cab full of little kids just so we could all climb out, fall around in the snow, and cry when we got cold. Party pooper. How dare he mess with my sacred cow? I finally talked Fred into buying a Christmas tree and "planting" it in a snowbank where it would be the kids' only possible selection. He agreed to this.

A short distance from the house, Fred found a canal bank covered with low, brownish brush, and stuck a beautiful little green pine tree right in the midst of it. Then we loaded up the kids and went looking for our tree. We actually lived about sixty or so miles from any naturally growing pine trees, so this little preplanted Christmas pine stuck out like a nun in a casino.

I think our plan worked the first year or two. Then finally one year we had children who were not so naive. We loaded up the kids, along with an ax (so it would seem authentic, of course) then drove v-e-r-y s-l-o-w-l-y past our preplanted pine tree. The kids spotted it and said, "There's one, but let's keep looking."

Keep looking? That wasn't supposed to happen. "No," I said, "I think this one looks great."

"Well, it looks kinda small," my son Homer countered. "Let's keep looking." Trust Homer to be looking for a redwood. Fred was too smart to argue with Homer, so he drove on down the canal bank another twenty minutes or so. No trees, only brush. Not even a dead tree in sight.

"Let's go up in the hills to look for a tree," Homer pressed.

"Um, no."

"Well, there aren't any good trees here," Homer insisted.

Eventually, we convinced the kids that we should go back for the one little green tree planted in the snowbank just to see if it might work. Fred and the kids got out to "chop down" our tree. Fred let the kids each take a whack at it with the ax and, sure enough, the tree toppled. As the tree fell, Jenny said, "Dad, what's that?" Fred looked to where she pointed and saw the red plastic tag that the tree-lot attendant had so helpfully attached when Fred bought the tree. I glared at Fred. *You forgot to take off the tag???*

"Uh—it's . . . uh, well . . ."

Yeah, Fred, this is fun now, isn't it?

I don't remember what he told Jenny. I don't know if he kept her in the dark that year or if he finally had to come clean. All I remember is that we quit hunting for preplanted trees. After that, Fred wanted to take the kids to the nearest tree lot, pick out a tree, buy the kids a soda pop on the way home, and call it good. (And when he got his way later, I don't think the kids missed the canal bank trek one bit.) But I couldn't admit defeat.

"You can't take them to a regular old tree lot for a Christmas tree," I told Fred as a last defense. "There's no Christmas memory made in a tree lot."

"Sure there is. They'll love it."

"They'll hate it."

"They'll love it. *You'll* hate it."

"I'll hate it," I agreed.

"You hate a lot of things."

It was true. And the list grew longer every year. So, you want to know what I hate?

I'll tell you anyway.

I hate not being able to re-create the memories for my children and grandchildren that were good for me. Why can't I do that? And why can't I sleep under the Christmas tree with them and help them snoop around with flashlights on Christmas morning while everyone's asleep? Why can't I make fudge like Grandma's? Why can't I spend a day or two making candy gifts for my neighbors? Why can't I pick out gifts for my family that they will like? And why won't the kids and Fred go Christmas caroling with me? I love caroling. I love the Christmas songs . . . except for "Frosty the Snowman," of course, because I never can get the words right. *No one* gets the words right, and we all just end up singing the chorus three times in a row. You know it's true.

I recited my hate list to my husband one year. He didn't completely understand, but he did his best to comfort me.

"Don't worry, Lynn. We have good Christmas memories."

"Yeah? What are they?"

"The Christmas Nativity that we act out is pretty funny."

"It's not supposed to be funny."

"Yeah, but you have to admit it's funny. The donkey nearly always bucks Mary off or sprouts a flat tire."

I remembered this all too clearly. (And I also remembered that when I was getting tense about the Nativity not coming off too smoothly, my daughter Rachel once advised, "Just let it happen, Mom.")

I took a deep breath and retorted, "That's because Homer is always the donkey. He thinks the story is about *him*. He does it just to make everyone laugh, and he's old enough to know better. He's twenty-six, for crying out loud. And angels are not supposed to stand on the back of the couch, either."

"Oh, Lynn, lighten up."

"That's it? That's all you've got? Don't we have any better Christmas memories than that? That's exactly what I mean, Fred. We need some *good* memories. We don't have good memories."

I fumed and sulked about this awhile, and then it finally hit me: I had turned into the grumpy men in sumo suits pushing the vehicle out of the snowbank, while Fred was the carefree passenger in the backseat with the picnic box, munching on walnuts and frosting (so to speak), just lettin' it all happen. His memories were just fine.

While I was yelling at people for not bringing the shovel and not pushing hard enough—or for bucking Mary off the donkey or doing angel summersaults—Fred had found a "peace" of heaven.

I resolved that this holiday season I would do my best to make a new start—moving from the huffing, puffing, barking-orders position to the "Hey, isn't this fun!" position. That is, I would try *not* to try so hard. Oh, sure I'd tell Homer he couldn't be the donkey anymore, and I'd get a chair for the angel to stand on, and this year I'd drag the fake tree out of its storage box in the garage because I've finally sunk that low. But I would not try to force spirituality. I would not try to force tender moments. I would not try to force tradition or some catawampus memory upon the kids.

Just when I had this all figured out, I got a call from my oldest daughter. "Mom, we're not coming to your house for Christmas Eve this year. We're going to start our own traditions because our kids are old enough now." No, no, say it isn't so! One of my sons would be at his fiancée's home, another son would be spending the holidays with his wife and her extended family, and my second daughter would likely be working. And where did that leave me? With the donkey and Fred.

On the phone with my daughter I was gracious and supportive. When I hung up, I cried. I had this all figured out now, but I was thirty years too late! I could do better this year, I was just sure I could, but I wouldn't have the chance to find out. Then I cried some more for my daughter. Oh, heaven help her—*what* slippery tradition or memory path would she take? How many years would it take her to figure it out?

I have no gift to pass onto you this Christmas, except this—the very best advice I have: Let go of your sacred cow. If you'll remember, Christmas and the whole nativity story are not about the cow—yours or anybody else's. I repeat—it's not about the cow. It's only about what's sacred. If you can let go of the cow, *peace on earth* will take on a whole new meaning.

The Greatest Miracle

Anita Stansfield

Christmas has always been a great event in my life. I come from a family of strong traditions, and my childhood memories of Christmas are tender and magical. To this day, Santa fills a sock with my name on it in the home where I grew up. (My father must have a great connection with the jolly old elf to maintain such a tradition for all these years!) My parents made the holidays fun and exciting while still keeping the real meaning of Christmas as the central focus. As a mother I have struggled to do all that my mother did to make a perfect holiday. I've learned that while my mother and I are very different women, the love she instilled in me for the Christmas season is a large part of who I am. Even in her absence, I strive to put my efforts into doing the things that will matter to my children when they are grown, just as the things she did now matter to me.

Following my mother's death in 1998, I learned what I'm certain everyone who has lost a loved one already knows: the holidays can be difficult to get through that first time you face the absence of a loved one who was once involved in your traditions and celebrations. As Latter-day Saints, we have a marvelous understanding of life and death, and we know that mortality is not the end. But being separated by the veil for an undetermined number of years is still a tough thing to face. Somehow we have to accept that our life—and our traditions—will never be quite the same.

The holidays that year *were* difficult, but I remember feeling a great deal of peace in spite of missing my mother. It had been her time to go, and I knew it. The nature of her illness had given us warning and time to prepare. The few previous years our family had put extra effort into making good memories, knowing that our mother's time on earth was likely nearing an end.

Years later, as October was coming to a close, I began to think about getting a head start on my Christmas shopping. I wondered how to handle all of the upcoming holiday preparations in the midst of a writing deadline and the busyness of family life. Every year I intend to do a little extra planning, to be ultra organized, and to avoid holiday stress. It rarely works out that way, but I do keep trying.

October twenty-eighth was a moody autumn day with gray skies and a not-so-brisk breeze clearing the trees of their few remaining leaves. I had a doctor's appointment and did some errands on the way home, then after supper I got back to the computer in hopes of getting some writing done before bedtime. My youngest daughter came to my room to tell me that someone was at the door to see me. I saved the file I was working in, walked down the stairs, and was startled to find two police officers standing just inside the front door. Two of my children and some of their friends were watching television in the same room. One of the officers quietly asked if we could speak where the children couldn't hear, and I guided them into the other room, mentally taking account of the whereabouts of my husband and children. Knowing they were all fine, I reasoned that whatever these people wanted couldn't be too serious. When they brought up my brother's name, I wondered if he was in some kind of trouble. I didn't expect to be told that he was dead. The most horrific aspect of that reality was that he'd taken his own life. With that news, I was hurled into a gamut of emotions unlike anything I had ever experienced.

The following days felt hazy—even nightmarish. At moments I would be fine and feel gratefully numb; at others, the pain was so profound I could barely breathe. I had grieved when I lost my mother to cancer. And I'd experienced many levels and types of grief vicariously through my writing. But I had never imagined emotions such as this.

On Halloween day, my siblings and I visited the cemetery to pick out a plot for our brother. Next we journeyed to the mortuary to make all of the other arrangements. We managed to joke a little about the irony of the date, and we were all grateful to have each other to hold on to.

The numbing effects of shock kept me going through the funeral, but the days following were too difficult to describe. About ten days following the news of my brother's death, I remember going to the grocery store, where I wandered from aisle to aisle, barely able to think enough to get what I needed, while the pain of my recent loss felt so tangible that I wondered why people passing by didn't stare at me with pity. Surely my grief was so consuming that it must have shown on my face. But everyone around me was apparently oblivious to my struggle to just complete the errand and get out of there before I completely lost control of myself. When the grocery clerk asked how I was doing, it took all my willpower not to shout out the truth. Instead I politely lied and said I was fine, then I went home and cried so hard that I was drained of all energy—not just emotionally, but physically as well.

Fortunately, such episodes were not frequent, but the time between them was constantly edged with pain as I struggled to understand how my brother's life—how any person's life—could come to this. I had studied suicide, and I'd written about it, so many of my loved ones turned to me for answers. I had some answers and was grateful for them; on an intellectual level, I knew the doctrines and principles of salvation and mercy, and I knew my brother well enough to understand what had led up to his action. But the pain I felt over his choice and my loss was still there. I gained a deeper understanding of how wide the chasm is between intellectually understanding something in your mind, and feeling it in your heart. I prayed daily for peace, strength, and hope, and I felt the Spirit buoy me up and comfort me, but still I struggled with the pain.

My husband and children had never shared close relationships with my brother, but they were compassionate to my grief. I did my best to grieve privately, however, not wanting my mood to put a pall over the household. As November progressed, holiday preparations felt more difficult than they ever had, but the constancy of my family's dependence on me kept life moving forward. I went through the motions and managed well enough, but my heartache continued. The shopping and decorating and finding the perfect tree all went on as if nothing in the world had changed. Thanksgiving Day was a successful celebration by most standards, but oh how I missed my brother! He'd never been very social or greatly involved with family gatherings during the years, but he'd frequently come to my home for Thanksgiving, and the stark reality of his absence made the occasion seem desolate. I feared that Christmas would be even more difficult. He'd always come to my home for dinner on Christmas Eve, and I couldn't help thinking of what gifts I would have given him. Instead, my sisters and I picked out a wreath for his grave. It all felt so wrong.

On a snowy afternoon, about halfway between Thanksgiving and Christmas, I was driving into town to do some tedious errands. As always through the holiday season, I was listening to Christmas music, but without my usual enthusiasm for it. I kept playing it anyway, hoping it would lift my spirits and inspire some tiny degree of excitement. All at once, without warning, the music seemed to come alive, filling the air around me while the lyrics consumed my mind and heart. I experienced a tangible warmth burning in my chest. And everything changed. I heard the words surround me surely as Isaiah must have heard them:

For unto us a Child is born, unto us a Son is given.

Because God so loved the world, and gave His Son for *us,* I knew that everything was all right. I knew in that moment that my brother was in a place where he could celebrate Christmas in ways I could never imagine. I knew he was progressing and happier than he'd felt through most of his troubled life. Most importantly, I knew that the Atonement of Jesus Christ applied not only to sin but to suffering as well. I had no comprehension of how such a great miracle worked; I only knew that it did. Peace replaced my pain instantly. That moment irrevocably changed me.

I missed having my brother at Christmas dinner, and I thought about him a lot through the holidays and in the months since. Occasionally, I feel sorrow at the separation between life and death, but I have felt the ongoing comfort of the Spirit, and the absolute knowledge has remained with me that my brother is well and that we will be together again. Even when occasional moments of grief creep up and surprise me, they never consume me. Since that moment of change, I have felt no pain over his death. My Savior answered my prayers and took that burden from me. No greater miracle has ever occurred in my life. But that's what Christmas is all about. It's not just a celebration of the birth of Jesus into this world; it's a celebration of His life, and of the knowledge we have that He suffered, He died, and He lived again—that He lives still.

On the anniversary of my brother's death, the living members of our family gathered in the temple to do work on his behalf that he could not do for himself. The peace we felt there was a clear contrast to all the pain and confusion we had experienced a year earlier.

Jesus Christ truly is the Prince of Peace. He offers His peace freely and abundantly. There can be no greater miracle than that.

A Gift for Jesus

Marilynne Todd Linford

A couple years ago at the BYU art museum, I saw a mural-sized painting—about seventeen feet wide by seven feet tall—by Brian Kershisnik. I sat and studied the setting and the figures of Mary, Joseph, the infant Jesus, two midwives, and a dog with her pups, all of which took up less than one-third of the giant canvas. I was delighted by the depiction, especially as my attention focused on the flowing throng of heavenly hosts that filled the rest of the painting. Angels of all ages were anxiously, joyfully—some tearfully, some jostling for a better view—observing the newborn Christ. I interpreted the angels to be premortal spirits who were able to witness and vicariously participate in this key moment in the world's history by observing through the veil. I wondered if the artist drew himself as one of the more prominent angels, maybe the big one elbowing his peers for a better view. Perhaps in pre-earth life there was a random selection process, or even a Conference Center–ticket distribution system, whereby some of us received the opportunity to be a spectator. Or perhaps we all had the chance to catch a glimpse of the long-heralded arrival.

I hoped I'd been able to witness the fulfillment of the prophecy that "there shall a new star arise, such an one as ye never have beheld" (Helaman 14:5). Although I wouldn't have been chosen for my current singing voice, I would have loved to be a member of the heavenly choir who sang the announcement of the Savior's birth: "Glory to God in the highest" (Luke 2:14). How I would have enjoyed watching Mary's and Joseph's faces when the Wise Men "opened their treasures . . . [and] presented unto [Christ] . . . gifts; gold, and frankincense, and myrrh" (Matthew 2:11).

As I sat pondering the ideas this painting kindled, I thought of Mary and the joyful gift she experienced as the Babe of Bethlehem was born. How much more joy she must have felt, years later, to see her Son as a glorified, resurrected being, the Savior of us all! I wondered if she knew in her lifetime that He visited His "other sheep" in what would become the American continent. How I would have loved to hover above that scene as reported in the book of 3 Nephi.

Somewhere along this domino trail of thought, I pondered on the fact that Mary's Son, Jesus Christ, has given me the greatest gifts I will ever receive: the gifts of the Atonement and Resurrection. I became conscious (I'm sure to a very limited degree) that I have been a recipient of His goodness and mercy at every stage of existence, from eons before His birth to eternities beyond His death. He has been the giver, and I have been the receiver.

I wondered, *Can a less-than-the-dust-of-the-earth human like me ever truly give anything back? Is it possible to give anything to Him who has everything and the capacity to give everything?*

I knew others had asked themselves this question. Two examples came to mind. First I thought of a poem by Christina Rossetti: "What can I give Him, Poor as I am? If I were a shepherd I would bring a lamb. If I were a Wise Man I would do my part, Yet what can I give Him? Give Him my heart" (In Jack M. Lyon and others, eds., *Best-Loved Poems of the LDS People,* 1996, 166–67). Next, I recalled Elder Neal A. Maxwell's suggestion: "As you submit your wills to God, you are giving Him the only thing you can actually give Him that is really yours to give" ("Remember How Merciful the Lord Hath Been, *Ensign,* May 2004, 46).

I naively wondered how such a gift could be significant in the vastness of eternity. What would it mean to Christ? Then a scripture in 3 Nephi came to mind, and I realized that such a gift had been received by the Lord in Book of Mormon lands long ago, when our Savior appeared to a group of people in the New World following His Resurrection.

After suffering the pains of Gethsemane and Golgotha, the Lord visited his "other sheep" in Bountiful, and in a beautiful gesture of His love, He healed all those with physical, emotional, or spiritual wounds (Alma 7:11). I pondered the people's response to this gift:

> They did all, both they who had been healed and they who were whole, bow down at his feet, and did worship him; and

as many as could come for the multitude did kiss his feet, insomuch that they did bathe his feet with their tears." (3 Nephi 17:10)

Some time after the people's expression of gratitude and reverence for their Savior, Jesus expressed sorrow as He recalled the contrasting cruelty and lack of faith He had experienced in Jerusalem. The scripture says He "groaned within himself, and said: Father, I am troubled because of the wickedness of the people of the house of Israel" (3 Nephi 17:14). Then He knelt and prayed words too sacred to record. "And the multitude did bear record . . . [that] the eye hath never seen, neither hath the ear heard, before, so great and marvelous things as we saw and heard Jesus speak unto the Father" (3 Nephi 17:15–16).

I thought of the disparity in experiences the Savior had had in Jerusalem and Bountiful. On one hand, the wickedness of the people of Jerusalem gave Him great sorrow. On the other hand, the righteousness of the people in the New World gave Him joy. Those who had mocked, scoffed, scourged, and nailed Him to the cross could not be more different from those who now bathed His feet with their tears. He wept for joy because of the righteousness of the people at Bountiful (see 3 Nephi 17:20–21).

Had I been a hovering, premortal spirit over this remarkable scene at the temple in Bountiful, I would have seen Jesus bid the multitude arise. I would have heard Him say, "Blessed are ye because of your faith. And now behold, *my joy is full*" (3 Nephi 17:20, emphasis added). Yes, mortals—mere mortals like you and me—can give the Savior of the world a gift. The faith-filled Nephites and Lamanites, by giving Him their loving hearts and obedient wills (both evidences of faith), gave Him joy! I like to think that if indeed I viewed that marvelous scene from beyond the veil, I also promised myself that when my turn on earth came, I would be a woman of faith who would also give Jesus Christ the gift of joy.

Angels Bending Near Earlene

Kerry Blair

I've seen Capra's It's a Wonderful Life *at least a dozen times, but I'd never experienced a holiday miracle of my own until one dark December night a few years ago. On that almost-Christmas Eve I encountered an angel—a couple of them, in fact—and learned a lesson in faith, prayer, and God's love that I will never forget. This is a true story. Only the names have been changed—but not all of them!*

"It's Christmas," I reminded myself under my breath. "Peace on earth. Goodwill to men." Supposing the heavenly exhortation extended to children as well, I looped the piece of cloth around a little shepherd's head instead of tying it around his mouth as I'd have liked to.

It was already December twenty-somethingth, and I had yet to bake a tray of cookies or wrap a single gift. Instead, I'd spent most of the month writing a Christmas pageant, assigning parts, sewing and refurbishing costumes, building a stable, affixing a star in the cultural hall firmament, and directing twenty-some kids who were all now sugar-filled and giddy at the thought of Santa's imminent arrival.

Despite being on the verge of a nervous breakdown, I was pleased. It was our night of nights at last, and we were ready. By the time the bishop stood to welcome the audience and announce the opening prayer, the set was decorated, the choir assembled, and the characters in place. Everyone and everything looked wonderful.

Having just completed my last task—shoving a crown on a wise guy's little head for the umpteenth time—I slumped against the wall in the back of the cultural hall to enjoy the fruits of my labors. Just then a door flew open and an excited, windblown little girl ran into the room and grabbed my hand with her icy fingers. It was Earlene. As if the name alone wasn't enough for a ten-year-old to contend with, this little girl was painfully thin, wore thick glasses, and had incredibly prominent teeth. She also had one of the strongest, sweetest personalities I'd ever encountered. I wondered if that was the reason she'd been sent to the family she had—one that seemed to have more than its share of trials in life.

"How do I look?" she asked breathlessly. "Where do I go for my part?"

She looked like she'd just tumbled off a hayride, but I didn't tell her that. Nor did I mention that she might have known what was going on if she'd made it to even one practice.

After assuring Earlene she looked beautiful, I nudged her toward a children's choir that was assembled around the piano. At least I tried to nudge her. She wouldn't move.

"No!" she cried, pushing her heavy glasses back up the bridge of her nose. "I'm an angel!"

People in the last few rows forgot that Brother Crawford was now pronouncing a blessing upon the proceedings and turned to look at us instead.

"You're not an angel," I whispered. I had no idea where she'd gotten the idea in the first place. Then I added encouragingly, "But you're a very important part of the choir." Never mind that she wouldn't know any of the songs since she attended Primary too seldom to learn them.

I'd dragged her about six inches closer to the choir before she yanked her hand from mine. "You said!" she insisted. "You said in church that I'm supposed to be an angel!"

My mouth opened, but no words came out of it. I was trying to remember just what I'd said to her and when. I seemed to recall speaking to Earlene in the hallway a couple of weeks previously. I'd been in a rush to get to Sunday School before my students and had practically knocked her into a wall. Whatever I had said then had been an apology . . . and perhaps a platitude.

"You said I'm an angel!" Earlene wailed.

As the audience uttered a resounding, "Amen!" I hoped it was in response to the end of the prayer.

I looked down into two myopic little eyes and knew it was possible—probable, even—that I had called Earlene an angel. But I certainly hadn't meant she was a Christmas-pageant angel. I'd meant she was a . . . well, you know.

Earlene didn't know. She only knew that since I was director of the pageant, God had given me the right to appoint little girls to be His heavenly messengers for ten or fifteen minutes in that particular ward on that particular night. Clearly, being chosen as an angel for the Christmas pageant—or believing that she had been—was the best thing that had ever happened in her short and surely difficult life.

Earlene clasped my hand again with both of hers, and her eyes shone. "I've asked Heavenly Father every night to help me be a perfect angel in His pageant. He *will* help me. I know He will."

The thought of Earlene's sweet, fervent prayers brought tears to my eyes, but there was nothing I could do. The pageant would begin any second. I prayed for words to explain to the little girl that she had misunderstood, but there were no words in any language that could fix this. No matter what I said, Earlene would still believe in her heart that God had handpicked her to be an angel.

She looked from me to the softly-lit stage and back again, wondering when I'd produce that white robe and silver garland worn by the other pageant angels.

At any moment, the welling in my eyes was going to run down my cheeks. There was no doubt in my mind that this misunderstanding would drive her parents even further from the Church. Worse, might the awful disappointment cause Earlene to wonder if God heard her prayers? Would she now wonder why, if God *did* hear her, He would ignore her hopes and happiness . . . and at Christmas?

Despite my fears of a family's impending apostasy and a child's crisis of faith, I simply didn't have an angel costume—or any way to come up with one in two minutes or less. My thoughts raced. Earlene wore a dirty orange sweatshirt and tattered blue jeans. No way could I slip her onstage with the robe-clad girls without evoking stares and giggles that would break her heart. I looked frantically around the room, hoping to spot a shirt or a sweater or anything white that I could strip off an unsuspecting ward member. While everybody looked festive, nobody looked angelic.

The Relief Society room was locked or I would have ripped the tablecloth out from under the pot of poinsettias and improvised. At that point I might have considered packing Earlene in snow, but we were in Arizona, so I didn't have any of that either.

Heedless of Longfellow's bells tolling despair back here in the corner, the pianist broke into "Joy to the World," and the first narrator entered. The play had begun.

An awful understanding began to creep onto Earlene's face. The census was going forth from Caesar Augustus, and she was going nowhere. "Hurry!" she said. "I need my costume now! I have to go be with the angels!"

I wanted to "go be with the angels" too, but my wish was metaphorical. I simply wanted to die before I had to witness the shattering of Earlene's heart.

Just then, Sister Morgan appeared in a doorway not six feet from where Earlene and I stood. If she had been the angel Moroni materializing with a golden trump in hand, I couldn't have been more surprised. In her hand was a hanger, and on the hanger was a clean, white angel costume that was exactly Earlene's size.

Earlene had her shoes off, her jeans rolled to the knees, and the robe on before I managed to draw a single breath. With a dazzling smile on her face, she raced across the room and hoisted herself onto the stage. Although clearly surprised at her sudden arrival, one of the "regular" angels ripped half the garland from her own belt and used it to adorn Earlene's long, hopelessly-tangled hair.

Angels are like that. Bless their little hearts.

When the program ended, I was still standing in the same spot, and I was crying in earnest. It was the best Christmas pageant ever. Mary and Joseph had made it all the way to Bethlehem without bickering as they had done in every rehearsal. The shepherds had neither dueled with their staffs nor played keep-away with their stuffed sheep. The Wise Men had found their way from the East without a detour to the drinking fountain. And above them all stood the angels—beautiful, bright, beatific—with Earlene in the very front. I will always believe there was a surreal glow—and maybe an extra angel or two—around her.

When I could speak again, I sought out Sister Morgan. Sue had no idea she'd just pulled off the biggest Christmas miracle since Clarence earned his wings. When I asked her where she'd come up with the costume, she reminded me that I'd given it to her daughter the year before. Only then did I remember being impressed to let the little girl keep the robe when she asked, but I certainly had never expected to see it again.

Several times during the year, Sue told me, she'd almost thrown away the angel costume, but something made her stuff it back in the closet instead of dropping it into the wastebasket. The same something had urged her to find it after dress rehearsal and wash and press it. In the end, she'd left it behind in her haste to get her children to the church on time, but that stubborn, blessed "something" intervened one last time. Sue had gotten up out of her seat, hurried home to grab the costume, and then returned just as the pageant began.

I was awestruck by the heavenly machinations. I had been prompted to give away a costume I wanted to keep. Sue had been impressed to keep a costume she didn't want. These minor miracles, set in place hundreds of days before, wouldn't impact the world. They were all for the benefit of one little girl—a child who loved her Heavenly Father and put her trust in Him. Because of her prayers, Earlene was a perfect angel that night. Or at least she was a pageant angel . . . with perfect faith.

The real miracle, of course, is the one of which prophets and apostles testify: the infinite love God has for each of His children. Elder Jeffrey R. Holland said, "I do not know exactly how He does it, but I testify to you that He knows us and loves us individually and that He hears our prayers. My testimony is that nothing in this universe is more important to Him than your hopes and happiness."[1]

I gained this testimony firsthand one beautiful, blessed near-Christmas night. Our Father—who loved us all enough to send His Son—loved odd little Earlene enough to send her an angel robe. He had known her prayers months and months before she uttered them and had set in motion a plan to reward her innocent faith before she exercised it.

And so it is with us. Each year when children sing, "Be near me, Lord Jesus, I ask thee to stay close by me forever, and love me, I pray," I feel the warm, prickling confirmation of the Spirit and think of Earlene. I don't know where she is now, but I suspect that she is still a

---

Holland, Jeffrey R., "Considering Covenants: Women, Men, Perspective, Promises," in Susette Fletcher Green and Dawn Hall Anderson, eds., *To Rejoice as Women, Talks from the 1994 Women's Conference* (Salt Lake City: Deseret Book Company, 1995), 96–97.

perfect angel, still close to her Heavenly Father, and still looked over and loved by He who blesses each of us so perfectly.

I like to think that Earlene still has her white robe. I gave it to her, of course. It's all she asked Santa for that night when she sat upon his lap. Besides, "something" told me that angel costume had been made and preserved and protected just for her.

Just *like* her.

Lighting the Christmas Fires

JONI HILTON

Have you every wanted to impress company with a perfectly Christmasized house?

My brother-in-law and his wife were honeymooning in Hawaii, when storms, cancelled excursions, and even crummy hotel pillows made them decide to return early and join Bob and me in Los Angeles. It was a week before Christmas, and I was more than nine months pregnant (which is why I'd had to miss their wedding in Mississippi). When the newlyweds called, I probably didn't sound very enthusiastic about their coming to visit, because what they didn't know was that Bob was already over *there* (announcing a game show in Hawaii) and was planning to surprise them as a "waiter" at a restaurant the following night. Quickly, I called Bob, and he wasted no time letting the couple know he was right next door. Suddenly, their honeymoon was fun again (spent with Bob)! But then they all hopped on a flight to Los Angeles. Little did my in-laws know that their honeymoon disasters had only just begun.

Their flight was delayed, so they wouldn't be arriving until 11:30 P.M. Nevertheless, I wanted them to come home to a cozy Christmas setting—a twinkling tree surrounded by gifts, sumptuous garlands, cinnamon simmering on the stove, Christmas music playing, and, of course, a roaring fire. Everything was perfect, and at 11:25 I decided to light the fire. This is one of the blondest things I have ever done. Bob had always been the fire builder—I'd never done it before. Nonetheless, I cranked on the gas, then went looking for the lighter-flicker thing. I found it a couple of minutes later and pointed it at the logs—then pulled the trigger.

KA-BOOM!

The entire room looked like a ball of flame. And it *was* a ball of flame, with me in the middle. The kids were asleep upstairs—thank goodness—and I somehow remembered to stop, drop, and roll. Which, at nine months pregnant, had to be a sight to see. I'll bet whales beach themselves with more grace than that.

I patted out the flames on my head and clothing, said a quick prayer of gratitude, then surveyed the damage. First of all, the room reeked of burnt everything. Second, my hair was coming off in solid, tarry chunks. Then I discovered that my eyebrows and lashes were gone, and my nose was bright red. Yeah, yeah, Rudolph. Blah, blah, blah. So we had a theme.

I went outside to finish pulling all the burned hair off my head, then went upstairs to shower. By now my scorched fingers and nose were killing me, so I decided to get ice packs and go to bed. First I wrote a note, though, trying to explain the crispy, partially-bald wife, who smelled like ashes and was upstairs in bed waiting for Bob. (Burned nose hairs reek for days, by the way.)

A half hour later, they arrived, and I heard a voice declare that it smelled like someone had been toasting marshmallows. I crept from around the corner with my ice packs, trying to hide my head (not easy), and admitted my goof, which could easily have put me on the Darwin Awards list. Everyone sympathized with my injuries, but we did laugh—how could we not?

At that moment, feeling sorry for myself and embarrassed by the state of my home, I caught sight of the nativity scene on the buffet. As I looked at that reminder of Christ's birth, it sunk in that cinnamon and fancy decorations really weren't the reason for the season, after all. My guests weren't here for the ambience; they were here to enjoy our company. Sometimes the Martha comes out in us instead of the Mary, and we almost forget that Christ—not Santa—is the center of Christmas. And I knew that Christ couldn't care less if I was missing my eyelashes—He loved me regardless. And this love is what Christmas is really about.

Eventually my in-laws' disastrous honeymoon ended in a happy marriage with only good memories and some great stories to tell about their honeymoon. But I'm still not taking any chances. I always let Bob light the Christmas fires.

Light of Life

GALE SEARS

The following is a true story, though fictionalized, as the experience belongs to a friend, and she is graciously allowing me to share it. All names have been changed.

Grumpy. That was the perfect word for the way Caroline Meyers was feeling. Not cross, or sad, or edgy. Nope. Grumpy. In fact, she was counting the days until Christmas was over. How grumpy was that?

Her eight-year-old, Julie, and five-year-old, Alice, had tried to talk her into a trip to the department store for a visit with Santa. No go. Put up a tree? Nope. Christmas cookie baking? Unthinkable. Caroline was seven and a half months pregnant and perpetually tired. She knew she should be the happy "Spirit of Christmas Present" rather than the cantankerous Mr. Scrooge trudging through the daily routine, but it was about all she could muster. This year Christmas just seemed like too much work.

Caroline's husband, Sam, stepped in to at least put the lights on the house (his job anyway) and take the girls to see Santa. He even proved somewhat efficient at cookie baking. Thankfully sugar cookies have frosting, so the dark brown of the overdone ones hardly showed at all.

The days moved along, and Sam put up the Christmas tree, which then sat undecorated; Julie and Alice took around the neighbor gifts (plates of their dad's Christmas cookies); Caroline's mom shopped for gifts for the girls; and Caroline went from feeling grumpy to lousy. She was missing Christmas—and she loved Christmas! And even worse, she knew that she was taking much of the joy of the season away from her family. Grinch.

One atypical morning, Caroline found herself the only one awake in a very quiet house. She picked up the scriptures and snuggled into

Sam's comfy recliner. When she opened the book it was to Luke chapter two—the Christmas story. Caroline smiled in spite of herself. She knew the words almost by heart. *And it came to pass in those days, that there went out a decree from Caesar Augustus, that all the world should be taxed.*

She read along with little thought or comprehension, the words skimming through her mind, but then her attention focused on verse five: *To be taxed with Mary his espoused wife, being great with child.*

Caroline glanced down at her own protruding abdomen. This was exactly how Mary had felt—more so, because she had been nine months along when she and Joseph had set out from Nazareth in the province of Galilee to tromp seventy miles to Bethlehem in the province of Judea. Seventy miles! And sweet, young Mary hadn't had any previous experience with pregnancy. This was her first baby, and here she was walking to Bethlehem (or riding on a donkey, which couldn't have been much better), nine months along and probably not being grumpy or even complaining to kind, concerned Joseph.

> *And so it was, that, while they were there, the days were accomplished that she should be delivered. And she brought forth her firstborn son, and wrapped him in swaddling clothes, and laid him in a manger; because there was no room for them in the inn.*

A light turned on in Caroline's soul. She saw herself walking the road to Bethlehem, grumpy about the Roman overlords, grumpy about the weather, grumpy about the smelly donkey. She bit her lip to keep from crying. Was this any way to honor the Savior's birth?

It was a week until Christmas.

Caroline found a small picture in a magazine of Mary on a donkey, cut it out, and taped it onto the calendar. Every day that passed, she would move the donkey closer to Christmas. If Mary could walk or ride twelve miles a day to Bethlehem and bring Christmas into the world with such grace and humility, then she, Caroline Meyers, could celebrate the blessed event with joy and optimism.

When Julie and Alice woke up and came into the living room, they found their mother halfway through trimming the Christmas tree. They hugged her and joined in the fun. Caroline resisted the urge to lie down on the couch and take a nap. Instead, she reached for another silver star to hang on a branch. She knew that trimming the tree, like most of her Christmas traditions, wasn't a necessity in honoring her Savior's birth, but she loved seeing the pleasure on her girls' faces as they joined her in this special, once-a-year-only event.

The following days were filled with activity—joyful activity that somehow edified her and drew her closer to her family instead of just tiring her out: cookie baking with the girls, present wrapping with Sam, buying and delivering gifts for Sub for Santa, setting up the manger scene in its honored place in the front yard, and attending the ward's nativity program where Julie and Alice were angels (of course).

After the lovely program, the Meyers family piled into the car to drive around and look at all the Christmas lights. It was one of their favorite traditions. Sam reached over and took Caroline's hand.

"Glad you could join the party," he said with a wink.

Caroline nodded. "Me too."

"Oh, look at that!" Julie squealed as they rounded the corner in an unexplored neighborhood. The house before them sparkled with thousands of white lights. They shimmered from the roofline, around the windows, and on every bush and tree in the front yard.

"Wow!" Sam said, blinking. "If I'm ever feeling light deprived, I'll just go stand in their driveway for a few minutes and soak up some rays."

"Dad," Julie said, clearly exasperated with her father's lack of true appreciation for the glistening spectacle. "Their whole house is shining with Christmas!"

It was a great truth. All the homes and businesses they'd seen—from those with simple candles in the windows, to multicolored wonderlands, to glimmering palaces of white—were all trying in their own way to bring some extra light into the world as humble symbols of the greater light that had come to earth.

Caroline recalled the glow of light she'd seen in the church windows and thought again of the nativity program. Usually her favorite carol by the angel choir was "Hark! The Herald Angels Sing." But this year it had been "O Little Town of Bethlehem." She'd closed her eyes and imagined tired Mary and Joseph searching for a place to stay in the crowded little village, then finally getting settled in the stable—journey's end at last. She'd thought about the donkey on her calendar, stepping toward Christmas day, and her own journey from Grinch to grateful. She'd even shed some tears when her angel girls sang:

Yet in thy dark streets shineth the everlasting Light.
The hopes and fears of all the years
Are met in thee tonight.

A little child was born in Bethlehem, whose life would fill the world with light—whose love would acknowledge and soothe all fears, heartaches, and even grumpiness.

I am the light of the world:
He that followeth me shall not walk in darkness,
But shall have the light of life.

Sam pulled over to the side of the road in front of a house with an inflated glowing snowman. "So, who's tired and ready to go home?"

"Not me!" the girls chimed in unison.

"Not me," Caroline answered with conviction.

Sam gave her a wry smile. "Really?"

"Really, Joseph. I can go at least another ten or twelve miles." She winked at the girls. "So put this donkey into gear and let's hit the road!"

Julie and Alice laughed. "Yeah, Dad." Alice giggled. "Get this donkey moving!"

As the car pulled out into the night, the Meyers family could be heard singing: "Joy to the world! The Lord is come!"

About the Authors

Lynn C. Jaynes

Lynn C. Jaynes attended Brigham Young University and the College of Southern Idaho long enough to learn that she didn't give a fig about college algebra or the history of costume. She brakes for pheasants and eats cookie dough plain. She is in denial about middle age, is resigned to skin wrinkles and thinning hair, and is wondering why the churchhouse is so darn cold on Sundays these days. She can't decide what she wants to be when she grows up; however, if the governor of Idaho gets to employ an in-house cook, she might consider that job—governor, that is.

Anita Stansfield

Anita Stansfield, the LDS market's number-one best-selling romance novelist, is a prolific and imaginative writer. Her novels have captivated and moved hundreds of thousands of readers, and she is a popular speaker for women's groups and in literary circles. She and her husband, Vince, are the parents of five children and grandparents of one and live in Alpine, Utah.

Marilynne Todd Linford

For Marilynne Todd Linford, Christmas makes winter survivable. As Mr. Tumnus says in *The Lion, the Witch and the Wardrobe,* "Always winter and never Christmas; think of that!" Having no Christmases would erase many of Marilynne's precious memories. Remembering Christmases as a child, a teen, a young mother, and now a grandmother brings her to the realization that the true and lasting reason for the season is Jesus Christ, because it is He who makes possible eternal life, where there is never winter but always Christmas. In whatever season of your life this Christmas is, may it be a merry one.

Kerry Blair

Kerry Blair is the author of eight novels, one book of creative nonfiction, and about two-dozen Christmas pageants. (She freely admits she's done her best work in the latter.) She is a born-and-bred Arizonan who hangs flip flops instead of stockings, would rather rollerblade than ice-skate, and has on more than one occasion bedecked a saguaro to rival any tree at the Rockefeller Center. Her most recent book is *Counting Blessings,* a book of essays and short stories much like "Angels Bending Near Earlene."

Joni Hilton

Joni Hilton is an award-winning playwright and the author of sixteen books. She holds a master of fine arts degree in professional writing from USC and is frequently published in major magazines. A former TV talk show host in Los Angeles, she is also a TV spokeswoman across the United States for various corporations and is highly in demand as a public speaker. Hilton writes for Music and the Spoken Word for the Mormon Tabernacle Choir and has been a columnist for *Meridian Magazine.* She is founder of Holy Cow, an organic line of cleaning products (holycowproducts.com) and is the winner of dozens of cooking contests. She is the mother of four children and currently serves as homemaking counselor in the Relief Society of her ward in northern California.

Gale Sears

Gale enjoys reading, visiting with friends, serving in her Primary calling, cooking, and doing historical research for her novels. Having grown up in Lake Tahoe, California, she understands the snow-filled magic of Christmas and cherishes the sacred feeling of the season. She lives in Utah with her husband, George, and they have two grown children, Shawn and Chandler. Gale's historical novels are *Autumn Sky, Until the Dawn,* and *Upon the Mountains.*